Happy Easter
Jesus Loves you

Alive
An Easter Story
By Kirthana J. Fanning
Illustrated by Jasmine Joseph

I dedicate this book to Mumma, for always being my strength.

"It's Easter!" Binky shouted, running
through their burrow.
"Our first hunt!" squealed Boba and Buno
behind her.
The little bunnies raced to their parents'
room, hopping onto their bed.

"Wake up!" The little bunnies shook their parents awake.
"It's nearly time for Bugga's speech!" said Binky.
"I'm excited to hear it finally," said Boba.
"Me too," cried Buno.

The bunnies of BunVille celebrated Easter each year with the Hoppiest Hunt, and Bugga, the mayor, would talk about the true meaning of Easter.

"Okie dokie," Mom laughed.
"Let's get a wiggle on then!" said Dad, jumping up.

The family went outside and joined the other bunnies heading towards the dwarf maple tree where Bugga stood. Binky, Boba, and Buno were among the first to arrive and sat at the front.

Once all the bunnies had gathered, Bugga cleared his throat. "Easter isn't just about bunnies and scavenger hunts," he began. "God loved the world so much that he sent his only son, Jesus, to earth so that those who believed in him would have eternal life."

The bunnies smiled, happy to hear those words.

"Jesus lived on Earth two thousand years ago," Bugga continued. "He was born in a manger, rode on a donkey, and fed a crowd with five loaves and two fishes."

"He was wise and compassionate and prayerful, oh so prayerful. But above all, Jesus was love. Everything he did was rooted in love. He performed amazing miracles. He cured the sick, fed the hungry, and raised the dead. There was nothing he couldn't do."

"Jesus was amazing, wasn't he?" said Boba.

"Yes, he was," agreed Bugga. "He taught everyone about God and how to love the Lord with all their heart, mind, and soul. To treat others the way we want to be treated and forgive others like God has forgiven us. People would come from all over to hear Jesus teach and be near him."

"Everyone must have liked him, right?"
asked Buno.

"Not everyone," said Bugga sadly. "Some people in Jerusalem, where Jesus lived, felt threatened by him. The leaders disliked his teachings and felt they were losing control of the people. They wanted to get rid of Jesus."

Bugga's words upset the bunnies. They grr-growled, sniff-snuff-snorted, and hiss-hissed at him.

"Settle down, everyone; let me finish," said Bugga. "Jesus chose twelve men from different backgrounds to be his disciples and friends. They loved him because they believed he was God's son. But then—"

"Did something bad happen?" cried Binky, anxious to hear what happens next.

"You're interrupting," said Bugga. "One man, Judas Iscariot, was corrupted by greed and betrayed Jesus for thirty pieces of silver. The soldiers took Jesus away and dressed him in a purple robe and a crown of thorns."

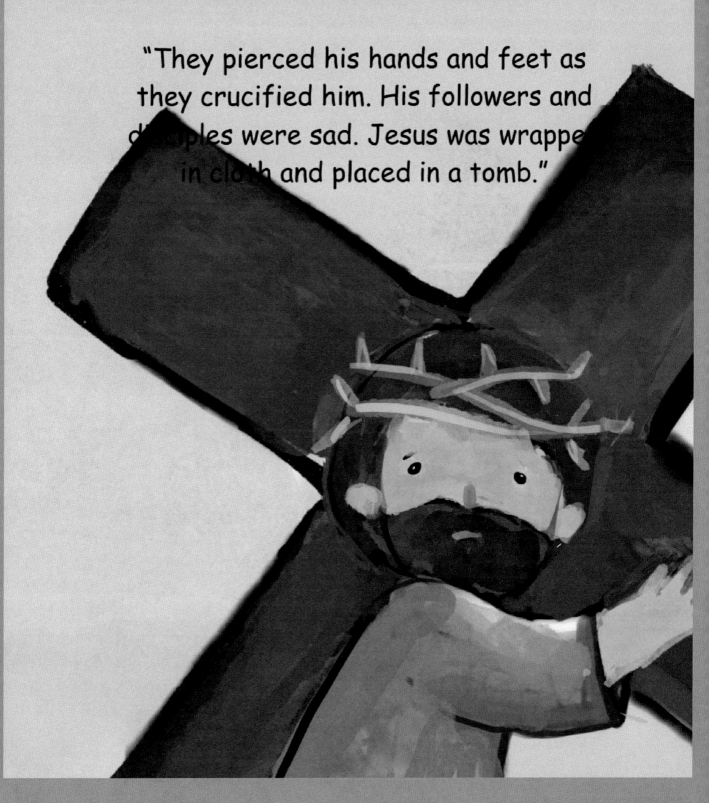

"And then?" gasped Binky.

"They pierced his hands and feet as they crucified him. His followers and disciples were sad. Jesus was wrapped in cloth and placed in a tomb."

"Oh no!" exclaimed the three little bunnies in a chorus.

"But something marvelous happened," Bugga said. "Three days later, his friends returned to the tomb and discovered the stone rolled away and an angel standing there, announcing that Jesus had risen. Then Jesus appeared to the disciples in all his glory and told them to tell the world that he is alive."

"Jesus is alive," cheered the bunnies,
filled with gratitude and joy.

"Easter is much more than bunnies and Hoppiest hunts," Bugga explained. "It's about hope and new beginnings. It's all about Jesus and his huge sacrifice." Bugga paused. "And now...the Hoppiest Hunt begins."

In a frenzy, the bunnies hopped around searching for treats. Boba found a bunch of carrots; Binky found a stack of strawberries, and Buno uncovered some blueberries. It was so much fun!

After the hunt, the bunnies spent
the rest of the day singing, dancing,
and laughing.

Later, the sunset turned the sky pink, purple, and orange, and the bunnies gathered to watch for a while.

They looked forward to the new season
and were grateful for their family,
friends, and home.

That night, they went to sleep with full bellies, happy to have spent Easter with their loved ones and knowing Jesus lives on in their hearts forever.

Just as Jesus lives in our hearts.

Manufactured by Amazon.ca
Bolton, ON

33340523R00021